Spirit Would Like You to Know

a colouring journal
to explore your soul

JANET SANDBERG

BALBOA.PRESS
A DIVISION OF HAY HOUSE

Balboa Press books may be ordered through booksellers or by contacting:

Balboa Press
A Division of Hay House
1663 Liberty Drive
Bloomington, IN 47403
www.balboapress.com
844-682-1282

Because of the dynamic nature of the Internet, any web addresses or links contained in this book may have changed since publication and may no longer be valid. The views expressed in this work are solely those of the author and do not necessarily reflect the views of the publisher, and the publisher hereby disclaims any responsibility for them.

The author of this book does not dispense medical advice or prescribe the use of any technique as a form of treatment for physical, emotional, or medical problems without the advice of a physician, either directly or indirectly. The intent of the author is only to offer information of a general nature to help you in your quest for emotional and spiritual well-being. In the event you use any of the information in this book for yourself, which is your constitutional right, the author and the publisher assume no responsibility for your actions.

Any people depicted in stock imagery provided by Getty Images are models, and such images are being used for illustrative purposes only.
Certain stock imagery © Getty Images.

Artwork by Betsy Reid

Print information available on the last page.

ISBN: 978-1-9822-5385-1 (sc)
ISBN: 978-1-9822-5387-5 (hc)
ISBN: 978-1-9822-5386-8 (e)

Library of Congress Control Number: 2020916418

Balboa Press rev. date: 08/29/2020

Welcome!

This journal is for you to explore and expand your inner self and get you know yourself on a soul level.

The intuitive message prompts are meant to serve as a loving nudge to move you forward in the direction of your dreams.

Consider each prompt, sit with it while you meditate and colour, and then write down what comes up for you.

My intention is for you to learn more about yourself so that you can grow, blossom and receive all the joy, love, success, and abundance that is available to you.

Love,

Janet

Spirit would like you to know that you are whole. Nothing has been taken from you and you are not broken. You have everything that you need within you and around you. Love yourself and have faith in your worthiness. It's never too late to gather yourself up. Return to soul — everything is right there, waiting for you.

_____

_____

_____

_____

_____

_____

_____

_____

_____

_____

Spirit would like you to know that you are safe. You may not feel certain or steady, but the Universe has your back. Trust, have faith, and know that everything is always working out for you. Breathe in calm and release anxiety. Surround yourself in love and light. Call upon your angels and spirit guides for protection. Use your voice to release your fears. Know that you are held in loving grace and kindness. You have everything you need to move through this. Trust yourself to know what you need and to turn away from that which you don't need.

_____

_____

_____

_____

_____

_____

_____

_____

_____

Spirit would like you to know that you must allow yourself to grieve. Being strong is admirable and necessary but you must also mourn and acknowledge what you have lost so that you can let it go. Do not let the loss take over and the strength harden you. Allow the sadness of losing what is no longer with you to move through you.

_____

_____

_____

_____

_____

_____

_____

_____

_____

_____

Spirit would like you to know that you have greatness within you, if only you would let it out. Holding it in will benefit no one. Be the powerful person and role model you were meant to be. Don't let others knock you down or hold you back. Trust yourself to be able to contain your strength. You are in control and can choose to grow at will. Don't be afraid of outgrowing your loved ones. You were put on Earth for a reason, so rise to that mission and embrace it.

_____

_____

_____

_____

_____

_____

_____

_____

_____

_____

Spirit would like you know that there are no second chances. All we have is the present moment. Enjoy it, take advantage of it, and use it to propel you forward. Your future depends on what you do with this moment, right now. Make decisions from a place of love and know that everything you choose is for your greatest and highest good, even if you can't see it yet.

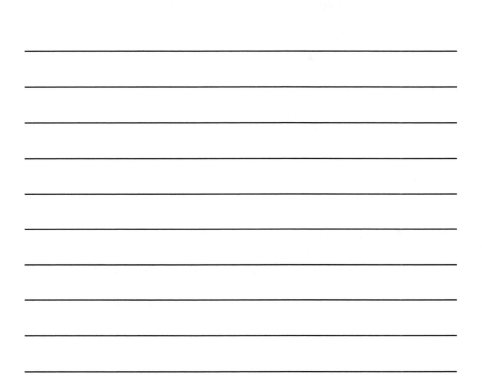

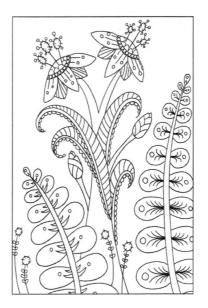

Spirit would like you to know that there are greener pastures ahead. Growth takes time. Health takes patience. Do not rush. Take small, incremental steps towards your goals. Do not fear the wildflowers in your green pasture. They may be unexpected, but they bring joy and provide extra benefits. Diversity is to be celebrated. Surprises often bring the most success.

_____

_____

_____

_____

_____

_____

_____

_____

_____

Spirit would like you to let your guard down. Open yourself to receive. A wall that keeps bad things out also keeps out the good. Soften. Trust. Reach. Grow. Be brave. Great things await on the other side of fear.

Spirit would like you to know that when the ground shakes, you are unmoved. Your rootedness and steadfastness give strength to those around you. But be sure to breathe and laugh. Be light despite your grounding. Allow movement and frivolity to balance your strength. Even a large tree can flower.

_____

_____

_____

_____

_____

_____

_____

_____

_____

_____

Spirit would like you to know that now is a great time for you. You are opening yourself and becoming one with the Universe. Trepidation and fear have no place now. Only Love. Love yourself for who you truly are. Love your gifts. You are divine. You are Love.

Spirit would like you to know that there's no time like the present. Don't wait. Don't linger. Now is as good a time as ever to step up and out. There is much uncertainty in the world and people need to know there is hope. You can be that voice. Reliable, solid, grounded. You are able to spread that message now, when people need it most. You are the calm that people are looking for.

Spirit would like you to rest. Worship yourself as divine. Accept no less from yourself than you would from others. You are a divine source of goodness - care for yourself as such. Be gentle and kind. Spoil yourself. You are worthy and deserving. Love yourself first.

Spirit would like you to know that the pieces are slowly falling into place, even if you can't see or sense it yet. Be patient. The Universe is conspiring with you, not against you. Everything is happening in the way it should, exactly on the correct timeline. Continue to take inspired action, rest when you need to, and align yourself with joy and nurturing. Breathe into your future and know that it is happening.

Spirit would like you to know that things sometimes do happen quickly. Do not try to slow them down. Always stay in flow with the Universe, even if that feels like losing control. Let go and enjoy the ride. Like floating down a river, look up at the sky and the treetops, rather than looking for potential rapids ahead.

_____

_____

_____

_____

_____

_____

_____

_____

_____

Spirit would like you to know that your strength is returning and filling you up. Feel into your strength and power, and harness it to create shifts. Let it flow so that you can lift others up. You have everything within you so let your inner strength do the work. Let if flow and let it be easy. Allow your strength to show.

_____

_____

_____

_____

_____

_____

_____

_____

_____

Spirit would like you to know that everything is happening as it should. Everything happens in perfect timing. You're not too late. It's never too late. All we have is the present moment. Embrace it and live large. Find the joy in every moment and never regret where you are right now.

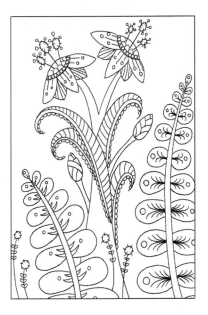

Spirit would like you to keep those vibes high! There is so much to be grateful for. Don't let those niggly worries steal your joy. Focus on appreciating what is. Visualize the big picture. Feel into the joy that you have and the amazing future you are creating with every feeling you choose to have right now in this moment.

Spirit would like you to know that there is strength in numbers. You don't have to do everything alone. It may feel like you are alone but you're not. Reach out. Ask for help. Vulnerability can be scary but it's so worth it. Find connections. You are not the only one feeling this way or going through this, even if it feels that way. Feel into your heart and ask who is one person you can reach out to and start there. Slow and steady. Be open to receive and you shall.

Spirit would like you to know that you are a gentle but strong leader. Lean into your leadership – with family, friends, and at work. Be the light and the voice for those who don't have the strength. Your calm and caring ways mean so much to those around you.

Spirit would like you to know that hard work doesn't always require effort. Let it be easy. You don't have to hustle and work against the grain. Let it flow. Don't force it. Take a moment to still yourself and your mind and ask how this could be easier. Don't feel guilty for ease and flow. You've worked hard enough. Don't make things more difficult than they need to be. Breathe. Let go. Ask for help. Be open to receive and open to ease. Let the idea germinate first. Don't force the flower to bloom before it's ready.

Spirit would like you to see the glory and divinity within yourself. See yourself sparkle like the stars that are a part of you. Rise up. Shine.

Spirit would like you to know that you are beautiful and whole. There is no part of you that is broken. You are exactly as you are meant to be. Love yourself. Embrace yourself exactly as you are. Be true to you.

_____

_____

_____

_____

_____

_____

_____

_____

_____

Spirit would like you to know that happiness is not a prerequisite for living. You create your own happiness. The old adage of thought-feeling-action is not always correct. Sometimes it needs to be thought-action-feeling. Create your own reality. Don't be afraid to show up and create what you wish to be true.

Spirit would like you to know that all things come to an end. Whether that's now or later, you can't begin something new without ending something old. Let go of what no longer serves you and rejoice in what does. We all evolve over time and need to constantly adjust what works for us and what doesn't. Change might hard, but sticking with things that no longer serve us is harder.

_____

_____

_____

_____

_____

_____

_____

_____

_____

Spirit would like you to know how strong you are. There is a mountain inside of you, strong and solid, that can withstand all kinds of destructive forces. Your strength is calm and grounded. It does not sway easily. You are greater than you believe. Your tallest peak is there for everyone around to see, and they will find you, and admire your beauty and steadfastness. Be the overnight success that took years to build.

Spirit would like you to seek joy every day. Old habits are hard to break but if you wish to change, you can. Focus on the present. One thought. One right action. Keep moving forward towards joy. Be open and expansive. Welcome new experiences. It's never too late to try something new.

_____

_____

_____

_____

_____

_____

_____

_____

_____

Spirit would like you to know that you are doing everything right. Your love and joy are coming forward. Actions speak louder than words. Be confident in all that you do and know that people are paying attention and noticing who the doers and the caretakers are. Don't give up hope. All is not lost. There will come a time when you will thrive. Stay true to yourself and you will get there sooner than you think.

_____

_____

_____

_____

_____

_____

_____

_____

_____

_____

Spirit would like you to do the work. The work is not what scares you but the results. There is nothing to fear. You are built for great things.

_____

_____

_____

_____

_____

_____

_____

_____

_____

_____

Spirit would like you to know that you are on fire! Rising up, staking your claim, and embracing your fullness. The time is now to show the world who you are and what you can do. Your light is so needed. Feed the flames and light up the darkness.

Spirit would like you to know that nothing lasts forever. Everything is temporary. Breathe and find joy in the moment. Then the next moment. Time is relative and not linear. Remember that you are in control of your thoughts, feelings, and actions at all times.

Spirit would like you to take a step back. Appreciate all that you have accomplished. Yes, there's always more to do but you have already done a great deal. Celebrate. Appreciate yourself and your hard work.

_____

_____

_____

_____

_____

_____

_____

_____

_____

_____

Printed in the United States
By Bookmasters